PRECIOUS MOMENTS

Joy to the World

Bianca Gascon

GIVEN TO

Christmas 2002

OCCASION

Dec. 25, 2002

DATE

LOVE, B

> "Behold, I bring you good tidings of great joy. . . ."
>
> Luke 2:10

Imagine that first, cold Christmas morning—the brightness of the night-time stars now dimmed only by the dawn's rippling rays. It is quiet, except for the soft sound of cattle grazing nearby, and the gentle coo and occasional cry from a newborn baby. The King of all creation has come—and has come as a little child.

Though two thousand years removed from that moment, we still celebrate the joy of Jesus' birth at Christmas. This year, before the food and festivities begin, enjoy the calm quiet of the morning as your family comes close to the Christ child through the loveable PRECIOUS MOMENTS® characters from renowned artist Sam Butcher. *Joy to the World* paints poignant scenes from the Christmas story with select Scripture portions that capture the essence of Christmas in soft, pastel color. The new tradition will take you back to that special day so long ago, and keep your family close for every Christmas to come.

"For God so loved
the world that He gave
His only begotten Son,
that whoever believes in Him
should not perish but have
everlasting life."

John 3:16

And having come in,
the angel said to her,
"Rejoice, highly favored
one, the Lord is with you;
blessed are you
among women!"

Luke 1:28

"And she will bring forth a Son, and you shall call His name JESUS, for He will save His people from their sins."

Matthew 1:21

And the Word became flesh
and dwelt among us,
and we beheld His glory,
the glory as of the
only begotten of the Father,
full of grace and truth.

John 1:14

"He will be great,
and will be called
the Son of the Highest;
and the Lord God will give
Him the throne of His
father David."

Luke 1:32

"Behold, I bring you good tidings of great joy which will be to all people. For there is born to you this day in the city of David a Savior, who is Christ the Lord."

Luke 2:10-11

"And this will be the sign to you: You will find a Babe wrapped in swaddling cloths, lying in a manger." . . . And they came with haste and found Mary and Joseph, and the Babe lying in a manger.

Luke 2:12, 16

"Glory to God
in the highest,
And on earth peace,
goodwill toward men!"

Luke 2:14

Sing to the LORD,
bless His name;
Proclaim the good news of
His salvation from day to day.
Declare His glory among
the nations, His wonders
among all peoples.

Psalm 96:2-3

Make a joyful shout
to the LORD, all you lands!
Serve the LORD with gladness;
Come before His

presence with

singing.

Psalm 100:1-2

Oh come, let us
worship and bow down;
Let us kneel before
the LORD our
Maker.

Psalm 95:6

Every good gift
and every perfect gift
is from above, and comes down
from the Father of lights,
with whom there is no variation
or shadow of turning.

James 1:17

Remember the words of the Lord Jesus, that He said, "It is more blessed to give than to receive."

Acts 20:35

Our first
Christmas
Together

This is the day
the LORD has made;
We will rejoice
and be glad in it.

Psalm 118:24

> "For God so loved the world
> that He gave His only begotten Son...."
>
> John 3:16

Don't worry. We don't have to match His gift. We never could. God asks only one thing of us, as He extends to us the greatest gift of all: receive it—receive Him. And in that package wrapped up before time you'll find all the love, forgiveness, and acceptance you will ever need. In addition, you actually become a part of God's own family, reserving the right to revel in your prize—Jesus Christ— from now until eternity.

This year, as your family gathers around the tree to exchange their gifts and delight in each other's company, remember Him. Remember the Unseen Guest, His unseen Gift, and give back to Him the only gift you can—your heart.